The Brew Beyond Brew

Reframing Coffee, Reframing Being

— One Cup at a Time

—

Kingfai Au

Tokyo, 2025

Contents

Before Coffee, There Was You

Coffee, as a practice of becoming.

Most people reach for coffee to wake up. I stayed because it reminded me what it means to be alive—not just alert.

I didn't grow up romanticizing coffee. It wasn't a family tradition, nor a symbol of sophistication. My early cups were functional, forgettable. But over time, something shifted. Not in the coffee—but in me. I began to notice that the way I brewed, tasted, and sat with it reflected something deeper than caffeine. It mirrored how I was learning to be present.

In a world driven by efficiency, coffee delays.

In a culture of constant motion, coffee marks a pause.

In lives shaped by noise, coffee offers a silent kind of structure.

4

Eventually, I came to understand: coffee is not just a drink—it's a **frame**. One that reveals your relationship to time, ritual, and self-permission. It teaches that not all energy comes from stimulation; some comes from attention. That not all flavor is sweetness; some is earned through patience.

This book is not a guide to brewing. It won't help you choose beans or master latte art. It's something else: a conversation with the self—held quietly over countless cups.

Each piece began as a small noticing: the weight of a mug, the sound of a grinder at dawn, the surprise of bitterness that felt more like honesty than offense. What emerged was a philosophy of pacing, not perfection. A record of ordinary mornings that somehow became portals.

If you've ever paused mid-sip—not for the taste, but because something inside you stilled—this book is for you. Not because we share the same preferences, but because coffee has shown us both how *tasting* can become *being*.

This is a book about presence.

And why it was never really about coffee to begin with.

Part I: More Than Just a Morning Habit

Reframing coffee as a state trigger— not a daily default.

At first glance, it looks like nothing.

Just a cup. A liquid. A start to the day.

You hold it without thinking. Sip it without pause.

You assume it's the coffee that wakes you.

But what if it's not?

What if the real function of your morning brew has nothing to do with caffeine—and everything to do with ritual? With the shift that happens not chemically, but psychologically? With the act of holding warmth, of entering slowness, of reclaiming space before the world enters?

We don't drink coffee just for the flavor or the jolt.

We drink it to signal something. To ourselves.

That *now*, we begin.

This section isn't about the taste of coffee.

It's about the space it opens.

The pause it permits.

The version of you that emerges—not because you're alert, but because you remembered how to arrive.

1.1 You Don't Drink Coffee. You Repeat Yourself.

Your routine isn't neutral—it's scripted by your past expectations.

You say it's just a habit.

A cup you make without thinking. A flavor you're used to. A morning motion that feels almost automatic. You drink the same thing, from the same mug, in the same way—day after day—and call it "preference."

But preference is rarely innocent.

It's memory, disguised as choice.

What you call your "taste" is often the echo of what once comforted you. Or impressed someone. Or matched a phase of your life you never fully left. That same dark roast? It may have once felt grown-up. That same oat milk latte? It may have made you feel seen. The sugar you don't skip? Maybe you've just never asked why it's still there.

We think we choose.

But most of the time, we're replaying.

And that's not inherently wrong. Repetition creates rhythm. Ritual. Anchoring. But when a pattern becomes too automatic, it starts to numb the very presence it was meant to support. The sip no longer speaks. It just confirms.

You tell yourself you're "not a morning person"—but is that your biology, or the

narrative you've rehearsed for a decade?
You reach for your coffee not because you
want it—but because not doing so would
make the morning feel unrecognizable.
You're not tasting the coffee anymore.
You're tasting certainty.

And certainty, for all its safety, has a price.

It dulls discovery.

It erases the question: *What do I actually
need today?*

Maybe today you don't need caffeine.

Maybe you need silence. Or movement. Or
stillness.

Maybe you need something warm that
doesn't rush you into productivity.

Maybe—just maybe—you need the
permission to change.

Because routine can be refuge. But it can
also be residue.

And if you never pause to question it, you'll keep calling old selves by your current name.

So the next time you sip that first cup, don't just ask, "Do I like this?"

Ask: *What version of me is showing up here again?*

And is it still the one I want to meet?

1.2 Caffeine Is Not the Awakening

What wakes you up isn't chemistry—it's context.

You think it's the caffeine.

That it hits your bloodstream, flicks a switch, and suddenly—*you're awake.*

But if that were true, any liquid stimulant would do the job.

There would be no difference between your morning coffee and a bitter energy drink chugged in fluorescent light.

But there *is* a difference.

And you can feel it.

Because coffee doesn't just wake your body.

It *positions* you.

It gives you a role, a rhythm, a re-entry point into the day.

It reintroduces you to yourself—not by force, but by familiarity. The warmth of the mug. The sound of the grinder. The first quiet sip before the inbox floods in. These aren't passive details. They're architectural. They *build* the moment.

Caffeine may agitate your nerves, but context shapes your consciousness.

That's why the same cup of coffee tastes different when you're alone versus with someone.

Different when you're on vacation versus late for work.

Different when brewed at home versus handed through a drive-thru window.

It's not the molecules that changed. It's the *meaning*.

We overestimate biology and underestimate framing.

Yes, your body reacts to caffeine—but that reaction is filtered through everything else:

Your mood.

Your memories.

Your expectations of what the next five minutes demand of you.

It's not about *what's in the cup*.

It's about *what the cup belongs to*.

Some mornings, that cup belongs to pressure.

Some, to peace.

Some, to distraction.

Some, to hope.

The same substance. Different signal.

And when people say, "I need my coffee to function," they're not wrong.

But the function isn't purely metabolic.

It's symbolic.

They need the ritual.

They need the *permission* to pause before entering performance.

They need a moment that says, *you're back—go on now, you're allowed to begin.*

That's not chemistry.

That's choreography.

And maybe this is why some of the most profound awakenings don't come from caffeine at all.

They come from *remembering*—

who you are,

what you want to feel,

and what version of life you're about to re-enter.

You drink coffee not because it changes you,

but because, in the right conditions, it helps you remember you have a choice.

To reframe the day.

To re-enter with intention.

To begin—not on autopilot, but on purpose.

That's not just a buzz.

That's awareness.

1.3 Convenience Doesn't Mean Careless

A cheap cup can hold sacred moments if you let it.

You hesitate to call it "good coffee."

It came from a machine.

It cost less than a dollar.

It wasn't single origin, wasn't slow brewed, wasn't ethically sourced in the way the marketing tells you it should be.

But still—

it warmed your hand, it calmed your breath,

and for a moment, it brought you back to yourself.

Why is that not enough?

We're taught to equate value with rarity.

To believe that only what's expensive, curated, and complex can be *meaningful*.

But that's not how presence works.

Presence isn't earned by price—it's invited by attention.

That convenience-store cup you picked up on the way to work?

It might've been the most honest thing in your day.

No pretense. No performance. No one watching.

Just you, and a moment that asked nothing of you but *to feel it.*

But instead of letting it count,

you dismiss it.

You scroll. You rush.

You tell yourself you'll "get a real coffee later."

As if "real" is something that only lives in craft and glassware.

As if flavor must come with an origin story.

As if a sacred experience requires the perfect setting to be permitted.

But coffee doesn't ask for permission to be sacred.

You do.

You decide whether to show up or not.

You decide whether the moment was disposable—or alive.

Carelessness isn't about the cup.

It's about the consciousness you bring to it.

Because everything becomes sacred

the moment you stop needing it to impress you.

And sometimes, the most overlooked sips are the ones that reach you deepest.

Not because they were designed to—but because you finally let something be *enough*.

So next time you grab that cheap cup from a vending machine, a gas station, a platform kiosk—don't rush past it.

Feel the weight. Smell the steam. Taste it without comparison.

You don't need more ceremony.

Just more awareness.

1.4 Drip, Not Drive

Pace is not about speed—it's about alignment.

We tend to think of time as a race.

You wake up already behind.

You make coffee like it's fuel—something to pour in quickly, to get you going, to catch up.

But coffee, when you really watch it brew, tells a different story.

Drip by drip.

Weight by weight.

The slowness *isn't waste.*

It's *precision.*

In hand-brewed coffee, every drop matters.

Not because it's dramatic, but because it's aligned. The grind size, the water temperature, the angle of the pour—they aren't about luxury. They're about respect.

A respect for the process, and for the moment that process allows to exist.

And yet, we don't apply that logic to ourselves.

We rush into the day, demand output before presence,

try to *drive* ourselves into function without waiting for alignment.

We want to move like machines.

But we're more like brews.

You can't force a good extraction.

You can't speed through clarity.

You have to let things settle.

You have to let the temperature meet the texture.

You have to give yourself to the process— and not just the result.

Because when you live only in drive mode,

you lose the nuances of your own rhythms.

You forget what it feels like to be *in pace*,
not just *in motion*.

And sometimes, alignment means not going
faster,

but going *with*—with your current state,
with the mood of the day, with the honest
bandwidth of your body.

Coffee doesn't scream.

It drips.

It waits.

It speaks in small amounts over time.

And somehow, that becomes enough.

Maybe your life wants to do the same.

So the next time you feel late, scattered,
panicked—

don't slam another espresso.

Don't press harder on the gas.

Try something strange:

Match your pace to your depth.
23

Not to what the world demands.

Not to what your calendar expects.

But to what your being actually has capacity
to give.

You're not a productivity engine.

You're a slow extraction, with hidden
complexity waiting for release.

But only if you're willing to drip—

before you drive.

1.5 You're Not Late. You're Just Unaligned.

Rushing isn't always about time.
Sometimes, it's disconnection.

You check the clock.

You curse under your breath.

You grab your coffee mid-pour, mid-thought, mid-self—already halfway out the door.

You tell yourself you're late.

But are you?

Or are you simply not in rhythm with what this moment actually requires?

Because lateness isn't always about minutes.

It's about mismatch.

Between your inner tempo and the world's external metronome.

Between how ready you feel and how fast you're being asked to move.

You're not running out of time.

You're just not where you are.

You're in the next email.

The traffic you haven't hit yet.

The meeting that starts in nine minutes.

The self-judgment that started in thirty seconds.

You're everywhere but here.

And when you're *everywhere*, even coffee can't find you.

You sip it in a hurry, burn your tongue, forget the taste.

You don't drink it—you *consume* it.

You treat presence like a luxury, when it's actually the doorway.

Because here's the truth:

Most of your rushing doesn't save you time.

It just fractures you.

You arrive scattered.

You speak from urgency instead of clarity.

You start reacting before you've even had a chance to feel where you are.

You're not too slow.

You're just too split.

And when you're split, you mistake adrenaline for readiness.

But readiness isn't a rush.

It's a return.

To breath.

To body.

To the rhythm of one thing done with full attention.

Even if it's just a sip of coffee, taken without apology.

Even if it means arriving one minute later— but entirely whole.

27

So next time you feel "behind," try asking:

What part of me am I not listening to?

Because being on time to someone else's clock

means nothing

if you're not *in time* with yourself.

Part II: Framing Taste, Framing Identity

Your preferences are mirrors. Every cup reflects you back.

You say you like it "this way."

You mean the roast, the brew method, the temperature, the milk ratio.

You've said it enough times that it feels like fact.

Like identity.

But what if it's not?

What if what you call "taste" is actually memory?

Or defense?

Or longing?

Because every preference lives in a context.

And every context is shaped by who you've had to be—

to belong,

to impress,

to feel safe.

That bitterness you say you love?

Maybe it once made you feel mature.

That sweetness you avoid?

Maybe it was once something you weren't allowed to want.

That "nothing fancy" cup you cling to?

Maybe it's not humility—but a resistance to being seen wanting more.

This part of the book isn't about judging what you like.

It's about *asking why you like it*.

It's about noticing when taste becomes armor.

And when identity gets brewed into your rituals without permission.

Because flavor isn't neutral.

And neither are you.

2.1 You Like It Because You Were Told To

Taste is trained. Most of your "likes" were inherited.

You think you made the choice.

You ordered the same thing you always do.

You liked it. Again.

You called it *your taste*—as if it came from inside you, as if it was yours from the beginning.

But what if it wasn't?

What if your taste was never purely personal, but accumulated—one comment, one commercial, one imitation at a time?

You liked what your parents drank.

Or what they disapproved of.

31

You copied what your friends ordered in high school.

You tried to like what someone cooler liked in college.

You forced yourself to tolerate bitterness because it looked adult.

You avoided sweetness because it felt embarrassing.

You started calling things "too much" when you learned you weren't supposed to want more.

You think your preference is a statement of self.

But often, it's just a map of how you've survived being seen.

Taste doesn't live in your tongue.

It lives in your memory.

And memory is social before it's sensory.

That's why the same drink can taste different depending on who's watching.

Why you suddenly crave something different when you travel.

Why coffee at home feels comforting, but at work, it feels performative.

We forget that taste is *highly programmable.*

It's shaped by culture, trends, shame, nostalgia, gender, class.

And once trained, it begins to self-reinforce.

You keep choosing what you've chosen, not because it's best—but because it's *yours.*

Or at least, it feels like yours.

And that illusion of agency is hard to let go.

But there's something freeing in noticing the pattern.

Because if your taste was shaped by the outside,

then maybe you can reshape it from the inside.

Not for rebellion.

33

Not for novelty.

But for clarity.

What do you actually enjoy—when no one's around to witness it?

What do you crave—when no one's there to validate it?

What part of your palate still belongs to someone else's approval?

You don't need to burn down your preferences.

You just need to *hold them up to the light*.

Ask: where did this come from?

And is it still true?

Because maybe what you like

isn't wrong—

but isn't free.

2.2 The First Sip Mirrors You Back

What tastes strong might just be honest.

You take a sip and recoil.

"Too bitter," you say.

"Too sour."

"Too strong."

Your face wrinkles, your hand pulls back, your judgment arrives fast.

But what if the coffee didn't do anything wrong?

What if it was just... honest?

Most people don't expect honesty from flavor.

They expect agreement.

They want the taste to cooperate—smooth, flattering, polite.

They want their morning brew to say,
"Here, let me make this easy for you."

But real things don't always come softened.

Some truths come hot.

Some complexity comes unfiltered.

And some flavors aren't here to charm you.

They're here to tell you how you meet
reality.

Because when you say "too strong," what
you often mean is, *I wasn't ready for that*.

Not just in your mouth—but in your mind.

You weren't ready for a flavor that didn't
bend.

That didn't seduce you first.

That didn't apologize for being bold.

You call it a "bad cup."

But maybe it's just an honest one.

And maybe your reaction isn't about the
coffee at all.

Maybe it's about your calibration.

How much surprise can you handle before labeling it wrong?

How quickly do you retreat from anything that resists immediate pleasure?

How conditioned have you become to expect sweetness—not just in flavor, but in life?

That first sip didn't offend you.

It just showed you where your limits are.

It mirrored your readiness, not its own rudeness.

It revealed your need for control.

It reflected the frame you carry into every experience:

"Please make this easy. Please make this pleasant. Please don't confront me."

But not all beauty is gentle.

Not all clarity comes warm.

Not all truth arrives with a smile.

Sometimes, it arrives as heat.

As edge.

As something that lingers longer than you expected—and asks you to deal with it.

So don't spit it out too fast.

That first uncomfortable sip might be the most honest thing you taste all week.

Not because it tells you about the bean.

But because it tells you about *you*.

2.3 You Don't Just Brew It. You Frame Yourself With It.

Your brewing method is a self-image, not just a process.

You say it's "just how you like your coffee."

French press.

AeroPress.

Single pour.

Espresso machine with calibrated pressure and precision timing.

Or maybe it's just the Nespresso pod you hit half-asleep.

But the method you choose each morning isn't just functional.

It's expressive.

You're not just making coffee.

You're making *a version of yourself*.

Each brewing choice carries a subtext.

The hand pour says: *I'm intentional.*

The moka pot says: *I'm classic, but unpretentious.*

The AeroPress says: *I'm in on the niche, but I don't need to brag.*

The café-order flat white says: *I like structure. I delegate. I keep things moving.*

Even the "whatever's available" says something: *I'm chill. I'm efficient. I don't need ritual to have identity.*

You think you're choosing based on taste.

But often, you're choosing based on narrative.

You're telling yourself—and others—who you are, without words.

You're broadcasting values, alignment, tempo, aspiration.

You're not just brewing.

You're framing.

And in high-performance, high-awareness cultures—especially in parts of Asia—this framing is not subconscious.

It's curated.

The method becomes a lifestyle signal.

The gear becomes a performance.

The bean becomes a badge.

Suddenly, your kitchen setup isn't about caffeine.

It's a declaration of your *sensory literacy*.

Your *aesthetic restraint*.

Your *ethical sourcing awareness*.

But here's the quiet danger:

When your brewing becomes a branding exercise,

you start optimizing for what it looks like—not what it feels like.

You perform a taste you've stopped actually perceiving.

And over time, the ritual that once grounded you becomes a routine that reinforces a version of yourself you don't even remember choosing.

So pause and ask:

What part of me is being reinforced by the way I make this cup?

Is it ease? Precision? Control? Image? Nostalgia?

Am I here for the coffee—or for who I get to be while making it?

There's no wrong answer.

But the asking keeps you free.

Because when brewing becomes framing,

and framing goes unnoticed,

you risk being locked into a version of you

that only ever wanted to be seen.

2.4 Cream and Sugar as a Story

Every addition is a small act of self-curation.

You don't just "add cream and sugar."

You adjust. You soften. You reshape the flavor into something more *you*.

Or at least, more like the version of you that feels acceptable today.

It's just a splash. Just a spoonful.

But behind that act, there's a quiet negotiation.

A story.

Maybe it started when black coffee felt too grown-up, too harsh.

Maybe someone once said you weren't a "real coffee drinker" unless you took it straight.

Maybe the bitterness reminded you of mornings you'd rather forget.

Maybe the sweetness reminded you of comfort you once had to earn.

You think you're modifying a drink.

But really, you're modifying *how the moment lands in you.*

Cream is not just cream.

It's buffer.

Sugar is not just sugar.

It's balm.

We rarely talk about how taste becomes a translation device—

between what the world offers,

and what our internal system is ready to receive.

Each addition is a way of saying:

Not like this. Not so raw. Not so direct.

It's you taking control.

Not to fake the experience,

but to make it survivable.

Or maybe, just... softer.

And that's not wrong.

That's *human*.

But it's also worth noticing:

At what point do your edits stop being about balance,

and start becoming avoidance?

What if you've never actually tasted the original?

What if you're sweetening a discomfort that needed to be felt—not fixed?

What if the harshness wasn't there to punish you—

but to mirror something you haven't been letting surface?

We all curate.

We all filter.

That's part of being alive.

But every act of addition carries a shape:

A preference, yes.

But also a fear.

A memory.

A message.

You don't have to stop sweetening your coffee.

But next time you do—

just ask:

What am I adjusting for?

And is it still about taste?

Or have I started editing the truth before I even hear it?

2.5 Instant Coffee is Still Coffee

Being simple doesn't mean being inferior.

You hesitate to admit it.

But sometimes, instant coffee just... works.

It's there when you're tired.

When you're sick.

When you're running late, or alone in a hotel room,

or camped in a moment where effort feels like too much to ask.

It dissolves fast.

Tastes familiar.

And delivers warmth when nothing else is available.

But still—

you apologize for it.

You call it "just instant."

You defend it before anyone attacks.

Because somewhere along the way,

you were taught that *ease equals lesser*.

That the good things should take time.

That flavor must be earned.

That if it's not complex, it's not worthy.

That if it came too quickly,

you probably settled.

But here's a truth most people won't say out loud:

You don't always need to be impressed.

Sometimes, you just need to feel held.

And instant coffee—however basic, however looked down upon—has a way of showing up when nothing else can.

It doesn't judge your state.

It doesn't demand your technique.

It doesn't ask you to perform being "someone who knows coffee."

It just says, *Here. This is enough. For now.*

And maybe that's not just convenience.

Maybe that's grace.

Because the value of a cup isn't in the gear,

or the origin,

or the Instagrammability.

It's in how honestly it meets you.

And sometimes, the most meaningful moments are the ones with the least performance.

You, in pajamas.

The kettle still heating.

Powder stirred into a chipped mug.

No witnesses.

No ceremony.

Just... presence.

So next time someone laughs at your freeze-dried fallback,

or you catch yourself judging your own cupboard—

remember:

It's still coffee.

It still counts.

It still held you once—

when nothing else did.

Part III: The Method is the Message

How you make it shapes what you think it is.

You think you're just brewing coffee.

But brewing is not neutral.

It has pace. Pressure. Posture. Intention.

And every one of those factors shapes how you *receive* what you're making.

You press a button, and it's utility.

You measure, pour, and time each drip, and it becomes care.

You froth, swirl, post, and tag—and suddenly it becomes identity.

But it's still coffee.

So what changed?

Not the substance.

The *frame*.

And framing doesn't just influence perception.

It *creates* meaning.

This part of the book is about method—not to rank them,

but to reveal how method itself is an extension of you.

How your hands say something.

How your routine tells a story.

How the way you treat the making affects the way you treat the made.

Because coffee doesn't exist apart from the way it's brought into being.

And neither do you.

3.1 You Judge the Tool Before the Taste

Technique isn't just utility—it's status, projection, and story.

You see the French press and think: rustic, unfussy, maybe a little analog.

You see the sleek espresso machine and think: professional, obsessive, expensive.

You see the AeroPress and think: quirky, minimalist, maybe trying too hard.

You see the drip bag and think: disposable, low-effort.

You see instant coffee and think... well, you've already made up your mind.

The coffee hasn't even touched your tongue.

But you've already tasted something.

Not flavor.

Framing.

Because tools don't just make coffee.

53

They make *meaning*.

And in a world where identity is constructed as much by aesthetics as by action, the brewing method becomes more than function. It becomes *signal*.

We tell ourselves we're just being practical.

That we chose our method because it's "what works."

But what works isn't just about efficiency—it's about self-image.

A machine that hums with barista-grade precision?

That tells the world you value control, mastery, maybe even prestige.

A pour-over ritual with glassware and gooseneck kettles?

That whispers patience, intentionality, design sense.

Even the battered moka pot you've used for a decade says something:

That you're loyal. Sentimental. Maybe quietly resistant to trends.

None of these readings are wrong.

But they *precede* the taste.

They shape it.

Because before coffee becomes sensation, it passes through interpretation.

And interpretation begins the moment you see the setup.

You're not just judging the drink.

You're judging the *person who made it*.

Sometimes, that person is someone else.

But more often, it's you.

You want your method to say something about you.

That you know what you're doing.

That you've done the research.

That you've earned the right to enjoy this.

But when identity clings too tightly to the tool,

you start using gear to compensate for presence.

You upgrade the machine, but not your attention.

You perfect the temperature, but forget to feel the act.

You chase the story *about* the taste—

instead of letting the taste write its own.

And over time, the tool becomes armor.

A way to filter out discomfort, surprise, even curiosity.

Because if your process is solid,

you don't have to question your relationship with the thing you're making.

But here's what gets lost:

Sometimes the most alive cups come from the "wrong" gear.

Sometimes the most honest moments are the least impressive.

Sometimes a flawed process makes room for a real experience—because the ego didn't get there first.

So the next time you reach for your preferred method, pause.

Notice what you're trying to say—

and to whom.

Is it really about the tool?

Or about who you hope to be when you use it?

Because coffee doesn't care how you made it.

But you do.

And that tells you everything.

3.2 Moka Pot vs Pour Over vs AeroPress

Every method brews a different self-performance.

You think you're choosing based on flavor.

But you're also choosing a *role*.

A role to play.

A posture to inhabit.

A version of self to summon and perform—one cup at a time.

Because the way you make your coffee doesn't just affect what's in the cup.

It affects how you *show up* to the making.

And that changes what the moment becomes.

The Moka Pot

Heavy. Familiar. Loud. Stubborn.

You set it on the stove like an heirloom.

No scale. No timer. No data.

Just intuition, memory, maybe even muscle memory passed down through someone else's kitchen.

It's not about precision.

It's about *presence*.

The Moka Pot is the method of someone who trusts themselves—

or someone who longs to.

It brews a self that says:

I'm grounded. I'm classic. I don't need digital feedback to know this is good.

But that comfort can become dogma.

A refusal to change.

A defense against nuance.

Sometimes, the Moka Pot says:

I've already decided who I am. Don't ask me to adjust.

59

The Pour Over

Clean. Minimal. Ritualized. Quietly obsessive.

This is the method of intention.

You heat the water just so.

You measure the grams, the bloom time, the spiral motion.

You center yourself in the repetition.

It's beautiful.

And in its precision, it offers peace.

But it also brews a self that says:

I am someone who does things properly. I take my time. I earn my clarity.

There's pride in that.

But sometimes, pride becomes performance.

You're no longer brewing for taste.

You're brewing to *prove you're the kind of person who brews this way.*

You frame yourself in control.

And call it calm.

The AeroPress

Unconventional. Mobile. Slightly rebellious.

You chose this because it doesn't follow the rules.

Because it looks like something between a lab device and a toy.

Because it's light, modular, flexible—like the self you want to believe in.

It's fast but deliberate.

Technical but playful.

The AeroPress brews a self that says:

I'm efficient, but I still care.

I'm a nerd, but in an approachable way.

61

I know what's up, but I'm not trying too hard.

(Except I kind of am.)

You bring it on trips.

You treat it like a secret handshake with other people who *get it*.

But even that—

is a frame.

A self-aware rebellion is still a performance.

It's just wearing sneakers instead of leather shoes.

You're Not Just Brewing—You're Becoming

What you use is never just about taste.

It's about how you want the world to see you.

And even more dangerously—

how you want *yourself* to see you.

Each method brews a story.

A tempo.

An archetype.

And that's not a problem.

Self-performance can be conscious, even generative.

But only if you *remember* that you're performing.

Because the moment you forget,

the frame becomes a cage.

You'll be stuck brewing coffee in a way that no longer matches who you're becoming—

but still clinging to who you used to be.

So next time you reach for your favorite tool, pause.

Not to change it—

but to *see it*.

Ask:

Who am I becoming when I brew this way?

And do I still want to be that version?

Because performance isn't fake.

It's just fragile.

Unless you make it conscious.

3.3 Espresso Isn't Bold. You Are.

Your interpretation of "strong" reveals your own thresholds.

It hits fast.

Small, dense, sharp.

You take one sip and feel your body tighten.

Eyes blink. Mind lifts. You mutter, "That's strong."

But what does *strong* really mean?

Does it refer to flavor? To caffeine content? To heat?

Or is it pointing to something harder to name—

something about *you*, and what you were expecting when that tiny cup met your mouth?

Espresso doesn't claim to be bold.

It simply is what it is.

65

It doesn't arrive softened.

It doesn't dilute itself to accommodate your hesitation.

It shows up as essence—extracted, compressed, unapologetic.

And the boldness you perceive?

That's your *reaction* to presence.

Not everyone flinches at intensity.

Some people crave it.

Some people feel seen by it.

Some people taste an espresso and say: *finally*.

So what does your "too strong" actually reveal?

Maybe it says you were calibrated for gentleness.

For things that unfold slowly.

For flavors that ask first.

Or maybe it shows how rarely you encounter anything that doesn't cater to you—

that doesn't sweeten itself, explain itself, or wait for your readiness.

Because we live in a culture of buffering.

Most experiences are padded.

Designed for ease.

Built to flatter.

Even the language of "bold" has been co-opted—used to describe branding, not substance.

So when something cuts through that softness—direct, unsmiling, clear—

you don't know what to do with it.

You call it "too much."

But what if it's just *clearer than you're used to?*

What if espresso isn't bold—

but you are, for sitting with it?

For letting that rush come.

For not diluting it.

For letting it speak in its own volume,
without asking it to lower its voice.

Intensity isn't aggression.

It's density.

It's presence that refused to spread itself
thin to make you comfortable.

And the real question is not: *Can I handle
it?*

The question is: *Can I listen without asking
it to change?*

There's something honest in what espresso
teaches us.

That a thing can be small, brief, simple—

and still shake something loose in you.

Because the strength isn't in the liquid.

It's in your willingness to *stay* with what that liquid activates.

You don't have to love it.

But if you flinch—

look at what inside you is tightening.

It might be your taste.

Or it might be your thresholds for truth, delivered hot and fast.

3.4 Every Cup is an Interface

Brewing isn't production. It's translation.

You think you're making coffee.

Grinding, pouring, waiting.

But you're not just making a drink—you're making a bridge.

An interface between you and the day.

Between your inner state and the outer world.

A cup of coffee isn't a finished object.

It's a moment you step into.

A field of connection.

A translation of raw materials—beans, water, heat—into something that speaks to your body, your mood, your needs.

And like any translation, it's never perfect.

Something is always lost.

Something is always added.

The method you choose is a lens.

The vessel you hold is a frame.

The ritual you follow is a language.

The Misunderstood Act of "Making"

Most people treat brewing like production.

A task.

A transaction.

Beans go in. Coffee comes out.

But a cup is not simply the sum of inputs.

It's a conversation.

The grind size changes the tone.

The water temperature shifts the mood.

The way you pour—hurried or slow, circular or erratic—imprints your state into the liquid.

You are not just preparing coffee.

You are preparing *yourself*.

The cup becomes an interface for how you are willing to show up:

Do you rush through, pressing buttons without noticing?

Do you pause, letting each step bring you back into your body?

Do you use the process to anchor a moment of presence, or do you outsource it to automation?

None of these approaches are wrong.

But they are telling.

Because every interface carries a philosophy, even when you don't name it.

Coffee as a Mirror of Translation

When you drink coffee made by someone else, you're not just tasting their recipe.

You're tasting *their choices*.

The way they like bitterness balanced against sweetness.

The way they interpret strength.

The way they decide what's "enough."

We rarely notice that every cup we drink is an interpretation.

Not just of beans or water—but of *values*.

One barista's "perfect balance" might feel weak to you.

Another's boldness might feel too heavy.

It's not about who's right.

It's about the tension between languages—yours and theirs—and the translation gap that lives between them.

And maybe that's the point.

73

To realize that coffee doesn't give you *truth*.

It gives you *perspective*.

It invites you to notice where your expectations clash with someone else's expression.

What You Bring to the Interface

A cup is never just a cup.

It's an interface that connects two frames:

the frame of what was made,

and the frame of who you are when you meet it.

You bring your hunger for warmth.

Your tiredness.

Your love of ritual.

Your preloaded ideas of "what good coffee should be."

You project.

You interpret.

You taste yourself as much as the drink.

And that's why "perfect coffee" doesn't exist.

Because perfection assumes neutrality.

But there is no neutral when it comes to interfaces.

A Question, Not an Answer

So what if you stopped asking, *Is this good?*

And started asking,

What does this cup translate for me today?

Is it translating calm?

Or control?

Nostalgia?

Or performance?

Because once you see the cup as an interface,
75

you stop trying to reduce it to "good or bad."

You start listening to what it's *telling* you.

Not just in taste—but in the way it connects you back to your state.

And maybe that's the whole point of making coffee in the first place.

Not to produce.

Not to optimize.

But to translate—

and be translated.

3.5 Filtered, But Still Real

Refinement doesn't erase essence. It reveals it.

You hesitate at the word "filtered."

It sounds sterile.

Controlled.

Manipulated.

You think of Instagram filters.

Corporate language.

Watered-down feelings.

And somewhere deep in you, a whisper:

If it's edited, it's not real.

But that's not how reality works.

And it's definitely not how coffee works.

Because coffee, too, is filtered.

Literally.

Paper, metal, mesh—whatever separates the grounds from the liquid—acts as a boundary. A translator. A shape.

Without that structure, the cup would be cloudy, gritty, unfinished.

You wouldn't get flavor.

You'd get chaos.

And yet—

the essence still comes through.

It always does.

We Mistake Raw for True

There's a modern suspicion toward anything that looks polished.

We associate refinement with performance, with hiding, with trying too hard.

We say we want "raw."

"Unfiltered."

"Authentic."

But often, what we really mean is:

Give me something that looks like effort wasn't involved.

We forget that effort can be a form of care.

That refinement can be an act of respect.

That choosing how to present something doesn't always mean faking it—

sometimes, it means *honoring it.*

And in coffee, as in life, structure is not the enemy of truth.

It's often the only way truth becomes perceptible.

Because clarity doesn't just emerge.

It's shaped.

What Gets Removed—And What Gets Seen

When you filter coffee, you're not removing "what matters."

You're removing noise—

so that what matters can actually be perceived.

The grounds stay behind.

The sediment rests.

The bitterness balances.

And what pours through is not less real—

but more *accessible*.

It doesn't mean it's weaker.

It means it's ready to meet you.

And the same is true for how we speak.

How we express emotion.

How we design experiences.

Filtering is not the same as censoring.

Refining is not the same as distorting.

There's an art to knowing what to leave behind,

so that what remains can land with clarity, with warmth, with depth.

Sometimes, rawness overwhelms.

Not because it's truer—

but because you weren't ready to hold it yet.

The Real Isn't Always Loud

Some people assume that if a moment doesn't shock you,

move you to tears,

or burn your throat—

then it must be fake.

But the most real things often arrive gently.

Like a well-balanced brew that doesn't scream for attention.

Like a sentence that feels inevitable instead of dramatic.

Like a presence that doesn't need to prove its depth.

Realness isn't volume.

It's coherence.

And coherence often emerges when you let go of the need to be "raw enough" to be taken seriously.

You don't need to bleed on the page to be honest.

You don't need to leave every word unedited to be real.

And your coffee doesn't need to be murky to prove its origin.

The Meta You Don't Say

There's a quiet intelligence in every filter—

a hidden choreography of separation and selection.

It doesn't ask for praise.

It just does its job:

make something experienceable, without diluting its core.

And maybe that's the real art.

Not to flaunt your depth,

but to *frame it well enough for it to be received.*

You don't have to choose between pure and polished.

You can be both.

You can speak clearly without betraying complexity.

You can brew with precision and still taste soul.

Because refinement isn't the opposite of essence.

It's what lets essence be shared.

Part IV: Time, Temperature, Transformation

Coffee teaches time differently—through heat, waiting, and letting go.

You don't boil coffee into being.

You let it steep.

You pour slowly.

You wait—not to pass time, but to *shape* it.

Because coffee doesn't reward urgency.

It reveals what only appears with heat, pause, and surrender.

This part isn't about patience as virtue.

It's about time as *texture*.

About how flavor changes—not by force,

but by alignment with unfolding.

Transformation isn't always dramatic.

Sometimes it's a quiet shift that only emerges if you stay long enough to notice.

And coffee—if you let it—shows you how.

4.1 Let It Cool. Let Yourself Cool.

Temperature is a dialogue. Not everything needs to burn to be real.

You lift the cup too soon.

The steam still rising.

The ceramic still humming with heat.

You sip. It burns.

Your tongue pulls back. You wince.

You mutter, *"Too hot."*

But was that a mistake?

Or was it a reminder?

Because coffee, like most things that matter, doesn't reach its best form immediately.

It needs time.

Time to settle.

To open.

To speak in a voice that won't scald you.

Heat isn't the enemy.

But it's not always the invitation.

Rushing Into Heat

We're trained to equate immediacy with value.

Hot = fresh = good.

The faster, the better. The hotter, the stronger.

Waiting is framed as inconvenience.

But if you only ever drink things at their hottest,

you never taste their depth.

Heat is intensity.

But intensity alone isn't flavor.

It's potential.

And potential needs pacing.

Letting coffee cool isn't about settling for less.

It's about tuning in to what more subtle layers might be waiting underneath the steam.

You're Not Weak for Needing Time

There's a hidden shame in saying, *"I'll wait."*

As if needing gentleness means you're fragile.

As if refusing immediacy means you lack drive.

But maybe it just means you understand timing.

Not everything needs to hit hard to be true.

Not every truth needs to arrive burning.

You don't have to scorch your mouth to prove you're present.

You don't have to rush into sensation to be awake.

Sometimes, waiting isn't delay.

It's respect.

For the thing.

For yourself.

Letting Temperature Teach You

Because temperature is not a fact.

It's a dialogue.

Between the thing being offered, and the body receiving it.

89

When coffee is too hot, it's not just your tongue that reacts.

It's your whole nervous system.

The clench. The withdrawal. The rush to judgment.

But when you pause—when you let the heat settle into something tolerable, breathable, receptive—

you begin to notice more than just taste.

You notice *texture*.

You notice *body*.

You notice what's been trying to reach you underneath the noise.

And suddenly, the same cup that once shouted now begins to whisper.

Not Everything Needs to Burn to Be Real

We've been taught that urgency equals authenticity.

That the raw, the loud, the immediate must be the deepest.

But urgency is often just proximity to overwhelm.

And some truths only emerge after the fire fades.

When the liquid isn't attacking you,

you can actually _listen_.

To the quiet notes.

The layered ones.

The things that don't arrive with a bang, but with a presence.

You've rushed enough in your life.

You've burned your tongue enough times.

You've forced feelings, decisions, performances to happen before they were ready.

Maybe now, it's time to let something—anything—cool.

Let your coffee cool.

Let your breath slow.

Let the moment arrive at a temperature your system can actually receive.

Not everything needs to burn to be real.

Some things only become real when you stop rushing to prove they're already there.

4.2 Extraction is an Art of Patience

Flavor unfolds with time—and so do you.

You want it fast.

You grind, you pour, you press—expecting the taste to appear all at once.

Strong. Obvious. Immediate.

But coffee doesn't give itself away like that.

Not if it's real.

Not if it has depth.

Not if there's something worth tasting.

Because flavor—true flavor—isn't a *burst*.

It's a *reveal*.

And reveals take time.

The Illusion of Immediate Clarity

You've been conditioned to expect instant understanding.

From people. From art. From yourself.

If something doesn't make sense right away,

you assume it's wrong.

If you don't like it at first sip,

you say it's bad.

But extraction doesn't work like that.

Not in coffee.

Not in life.

Extraction is a slow unfolding of potential.

Each second reshapes the flavor.

Too fast, and the taste is flat—
underdeveloped.

Too long, and bitterness overshadows subtlety.

To get it _right_,

you don't just need attention.

You need patience.

And most people aren't trained for that.

Your Taste Evolves in Real Time

What you taste isn't just the liquid.

It's your perception catching up to the process.

At first, you get acidity.

Then something floral.

Then weight, structure, a hint of something you can't name.

Your tongue doesn't decode it instantly.

Your memory struggles to assign labels.

And that's the point.

Because good coffee—and good experience—doesn't always fit into the categories you've rehearsed.

95

You have to *sit with it*.

Let it change.

Let *you* change.

Because you're not a static taster.

You're an extractor too.

You extract meaning from experience the same way water extracts flavor from the grounds—

through pressure, contact, duration.

Why Patience Is So Hard

Patience isn't just about waiting.

It's about *staying open while you wait*.

That's why most people would rather over-extract and move on,

than wait for something they don't yet understand.

They'd rather *decide quickly*,

than feel uncertain.

But you don't get to taste the full story if you can't tolerate the silence in between.

Every great cup passes through a phase of "not quite."

Of "almost."

Of "I don't know yet."

And if you can't stand that ambiguity,

you'll miss the note that only appears in the final seconds.

You'll miss *yourself*—right before you would've arrived.

What This Says About You

Because the way you extract your coffee

reveals the way you extract everything else.

Are you in a hurry to get to the result?

Do you push harder when it doesn't taste "ready"?

Do you trust the process—or do you constantly tweak, adjust, overcorrect?

Do you *let something come to you*,

or do you try to force it out before it's ripe?

Coffee doesn't reward impatience.

Neither does insight.

Neither does growth.

What you want isn't hidden.

It's just... unfolding.

But only if you let it.

The Taste Arrives When You Do

So next time you brew, notice your hands.

Your timing.

Your breath.

Notice when you start to rush.

Notice when you stop believing something's happening just because you can't see it yet.

And then—wait.

Let the water fall.

Let the moment bloom.

Let yourself *arrive*.

Because flavor unfolds with time.

And so do you.

4.3 The Bean That Traveled Further Than You

Every sip is a migration story you didn't notice.

You hold the cup.

Steam rising.

The smell feels close—familiar, maybe even intimate.

But what you're tasting didn't come from here.

It came from far.

From lands you've never walked.

From hands you'll never meet.

That warmth between your palms is the end of a journey—

a journey you rarely think about.

Because coffee doesn't just *appear*.

It *arrives*.

And it brings with it a story you weren't listening for.

Invisible Labor, Intangible Distance

The beans were grown on a hillside in Guatemala.

Or Ethiopia.

Or Sumatra.

Picked by hands that started work before sunrise.

Dried in sun that felt different from yours.

Bagged. Traded. Roasted across continents.

Ground and brewed in your quiet kitchen.

You call it *your* coffee.

But none of it began with you.

You sip it in silence.

You thank no one.

101

Because the system was designed to make you feel like it's yours.

Like ownership is natural.

Like access is default.

But it's not.

It's history, logistics, power, extraction—

all wrapped in the illusion of convenience.

The Politics of Proximity

You feel close to the flavor.

But you're far from the source.

And that distance isn't just physical.

It's cognitive.

The cup flattens the journey.

Compresses it.

Makes something *migrated* feel *immediate*.

Something *translated* feel *personal*.

But if you were to trace the steps backward,

you'd realize how many lives, climates, currencies, and decisions had to align—

just to create this one moment of warmth on your lips.

You didn't drink coffee.

You drank a global choreography.

You Live in a System of Hidden Migrations

And it's not just coffee.

Every shirt.

Every screen.

Every sentence spoken in a language not yours.

You're surrounded by artifacts of movement—

of things and people and cultures that left somewhere to arrive here,

packaged, polished, made palatable.

And just like coffee,

you consume them without noticing their path.

But every object you hold contains an echo:

of dislocation,

of resilience,

of exchange.

And when you say, "This is my taste,"

you're not wrong.

But it's a taste built on pathways you didn't walk.

And someone else did.

What This Says About You

It's not guilt.

It's not blame.

It's awareness.

To see that your flavor is never isolated.

That your preference is woven into systems.

That every sip you love was made possible by movements—both human and mechanical—you were never taught to feel.

And once you start to notice...

You feel it.

The weight of the cup changes.

The heat lingers longer.

The taste deepens—because now it has *distance* in it.

It becomes not just *your coffee*,

but a point of contact between lives.

From Mouth to Map

So next time you sip, pause.

Not to moralize.

Not to perform mindfulness.

But to quietly ask:

Where did this come from?

Who did it pass through?

And what does it mean that it landed in my hands, right now, in this version of the world?

Because even if you never leave your city—

this cup traveled further than you.

And maybe, if you listen carefully,

it might still be on its way through you—

becoming part of *your* story now,

not as the owner,

but as the next carrier of meaning.

4.4 Bitterness Evolves, If You Stay

What feels harsh might be a lesson in disguise.

You taste it.

That sharp edge. That refusal to please.

That moment where your mouth tightens, your brow furrows,

and you think: *I don't like this*.

You call it bitter.

And you almost push the cup away.

Because bitterness is coded as rejection.

As a warning.

As something we were taught to avoid.

But what if that first reaction was just... an opening?

Not to danger—

but to *depth*?

You Were Taught to Move Away

From your earliest days, you learned that pleasant meant good.

Sweet meant safe.

Harsh meant wrong.

You praised the drinks that were smooth.

You smiled at flavors that gave you something quickly.

You leaned toward the easy, the familiar, the immediately enjoyable.

And you moved away from what challenged your palate.

From what lingered, what burned, what made you work.

But coffee—real coffee—doesn't always show up with a smile.

Sometimes it shows up as a mirror,

revealing the thresholds you never questioned.

And bitterness...

is often the first note of honesty.

Bitterness Is Not the Enemy. It's the Threshold.

In the first sip, bitterness feels like resistance.

But stay with it.

Let it move. Let it settle. Let it unfold.

Suddenly, it shifts.

It opens into weight.

Into structure.

Into the foundation that makes every other flavor legible.

Without bitterness, the sweetness feels shallow.

109

Without contrast, the complexity flattens.

Bitterness isn't the problem.

It's the test.

The invitation.

And like most invitations to growth,

it arrives in a language you weren't taught
to trust.

**Why You Flee (And Why You Might Stay)**

When something bitter touches you,

your first impulse is to leave.

To sip something easier.

To go back to what doesn't ask as much.

To stay comfortable.

But growth doesn't live in comfort.

It lives in _tolerance—_

in your willingness to stay just a little longer with what unsettles you.

And not just in coffee.

In feedback.

In grief.

In boredom.

In silence.

Bitterness shows up in all these places.

And if you leave too quickly,

you miss what it was trying to show you.

Because what starts as harsh

often ends as clarity.

But only for those who stay.

Bitterness as a Structural Signal

Bitterness is structural.

It tells you about density.

It tells you about pressure—what the bean lived through,

what the roast exposed,

what the brew emphasized.

And isn't that true for people, too?

The bitterness in a person's voice

often comes from compression—

of years, of silence, of having to hold too much for too long.

If you leave too soon,

you only ever meet the outer edge.

But if you stay—

with kindness, with patience, with attention—

you start to taste the story inside.

It's the same with coffee.

The Evolution Only Happens With
You

Bitterness doesn't evolve on its own.

It evolves _in relationship_—

through your nervous system,

your expectations,

your willingness to keep tasting even after discomfort begins.

It softens not because it changes,

but because _you_ do.

You build tolerance.

You expand your flavor vocabulary.

You remember that what begins as rejection

might end as revelation.

So the next time you flinch at bitterness—

in a cup, in a conversation, in a memory—

don't turn away just yet.

Wait.

Stay.

Feel.

Bitterness isn't always beautiful.

But sometimes, it's true.

And truth, like flavor, takes time to be received.

4.5 You Taste Time, Not Just Beans

Memory, origin, and waiting all dissolve into that cup.

You think you're tasting a bean.

A region.

A roast.

Something grown somewhere distant and processed somewhere closer.

But that's not all.

You're tasting waiting.

Aging.

Timing.

You're tasting the moment *after* the thing was ready—

not the moment it was made.

Because coffee, like people, doesn't arrive raw.

It arrives *conditioned by time.*

And time is not passive.

It reshapes everything it touches.

The Bean Wasn't Always Ready

When it was first picked, it wasn't
drinkable.

It had to dry.

To be milled.

To rest.

To be roasted.

To rest *again.*

Then ground.

Then brewed.

Each phase a conversation with time.

Each pause a negotiation between flavor
and readiness.

And at every stage, someone had to decide:

Now, not yet.

Wait longer.

Hold back.

You're not just sipping what grew.

You're sipping what *was allowed to become.*

What You Taste Is Time's Signature

That nutty warmth?

That acidity?

That smoothness?

They're not just about the soil.

They're about *sequence.*

How long the roast lasted.

How hot the water was.

117

How slowly the pour happened.

How much space was given for the hidden parts of the flavor to emerge.

And that's true for more than coffee.

Every meaningful thing you experience

carries time's fingerprint—

not as a timestamp,

but as a texture.

You feel it in the pause before a friend responds.

In the silence between notes in music.

In the breath someone takes before telling you something they've never said.

We don't just taste objects.

We taste unfolding.

Memory Isn't Separate—It's Steeped In

You taste something and say:

This reminds me of that trip.

Of that person.

Of that morning when everything finally made sense.

That isn't nostalgia.

That's _structure_.

Memory attaches itself to sensory anchors.

And coffee is one of the most fertile grounds for memory to root itself.

Not just because of smell,

but because of _time-density_.

You don't remember every cup.

You remember the ones that held _you_—

in transition,

in grief,

119

in joy,

in presence.

Those cups are still inside you.

Still unfolding.

You're Not Tasting the Present

You think this cup is now.

But it isn't.

It's weeks of logistics.

Months of tending.

Years of weather patterns.

Decades of regional history.

Generations of taste.

And you—

you are the last step in that timeline.

Not the center.

Just the one who receives.

But that's not a demotion.

It's a reminder:

That meaning doesn't have to start with you

to be *for* you.

And sometimes, the most real thing you can do

is *receive*—fully.

Time, Tasted

So next time you say, *This coffee tastes deep,*

ask yourself:

What part of that depth is actually flavor—

and what part is time?

Time, condensed.

Time, resolved.

Time, made drinkable.

Because the truth is, you're not just tasting coffee.

You're tasting what patience made possible.

What memory let survive.

What origin refused to rush.

You taste time.

And if you let it,

time tastes you back.

Part V: Solitude, Presence, and Connection

Coffee isn't just what you drink. It's how you relate.

Some cups are shared.

Some aren't.

But even when you drink alone,

you're not alone in the experience.

Because coffee is never just liquid.

It's *interface*.

Between you and your thoughts.

Between you and the person across from you.

Between your inner tempo and the world's expectations.

This part isn't about social rituals or coffee dates.

It's about how we show up—

123

to ourselves,

to each other,

to the invisible space in between.

And how a single sip can remind you:

You're not just a drinker.

You're a participant in presence.

5.1 Drinking Alone Is Not Lonely

Solitude can be a presence, not a gap.

You sit with your cup.

No conversation.

No music.

No audience.

Just you and the sound of your own breath.

Someone else might call this empty.

You don't.

Because you've been here before—

in this quiet,

in this unhurried stillness,

where nothing needs to happen,

and somehow, everything does.

Not All Silence Is Absence

We live in a culture that mistrusts quiet.

If there's no talking, no productivity, no interaction—

we call it void.

But solitude isn't the absence of connection.

It's the *return to self*.

And coffee, in its simplest form, offers that return.

A cup that doesn't demand.

That doesn't measure your worth by output.

That doesn't perform intimacy—

but holds space for it.

You don't need someone across the table to feel anchored.

Sometimes, you just need a moment that lets you *be*.

You're Not Performing Here

Most of the time, you drink coffee *with* a role.

The colleague.

The date.

The friend.

The guest.

You pick the drink to match the context.

You filter your expression.

You mirror the energy across from you.

126

But when you're alone—

truly alone—

you stop doing that.

And what's left?

Not loneliness.

But *unmasked presence.*

Not the absence of connection,

but the rebalancing of how much
connection to the external world you
actually need.

The noise lowers.

The inner voice shifts.

And the flavor of the coffee becomes more
than taste—

it becomes *texture in time.*

The Meta You Forget to Notice

This stillness is not neutral.

127

It's generative.

It's a system recalibrating.

A nervous system re-centering.

A self, briefly, no longer outsourced to reaction.

You think you're just "drinking by yourself."

But you're actually participating in a kind of micro-ritual—

one that doesn't ask for witnesses,

but still reshapes you.

You're not watching.

You're *being*.

And there's a kind of honesty in that

that no interaction can replicate.

Solitude Is a Form of Relationship

You can only be truly with others

to the extent that you can be truly with yourself.

This isn't a moral claim.

It's a *relational truth*.

Because if you rush to fill every silence,

you lose your own texture.

If you can't sit through one quiet cup,

you will carry that hunger into every dialogue—

pulling, proving, projecting.

But if you can hold this moment alone—

and let it hold you—

then what you bring back to others

won't be a need.

It will be *presence*.

You're Not Alone in the Room

Even now, in this silence,

you're not truly alone.

The warmth of the mug.

The aroma in the air.

The trace of thoughts emerging and
dissolving.

The invisible architecture of who you are
when no one's watching.

You're in dialogue with something.

Maybe the self you're becoming.

Maybe the life you've built around this
pause.

Maybe the moment itself.

So next time you sit with a cup and no one
else—

don't call it lonely too fast.

You might be in the most honest company you've had all week.

And the coffee?

It's not just filling the space.

It's *holding it*.

5.2 Coffee Dates Aren't About Coffee

You're not sharing caffeine. You're sharing attention.

There's a drink on the table.

But no one's really tasting it.

Not with their tongue.

Not in the sensory way, at least.

The espresso cools.

The latte art fades.

The aroma escapes before anyone notices.

Because in a coffee date—

what you drink isn't the point.

What you pour...

is attention.

The Cup is an Excuse

You don't ask someone,

"Would you like to share 47 minutes of undivided presence?"

You ask,

"Wanna grab coffee?"

It's easier that way.

The drink is a pretext—

a structure that legitimizes pause.

A placeholder for unsaid intentions.

A neutral container to hold the weight of attention

without making it too obvious.

You're not really here for the caffeine.

You're here to look someone in the eye

and feel that you both still exist.

The cup is warm.

But it's the other person's presence

that keeps you from cooling.

What You're Really Consuming

In that moment—two hands on cups,

two voices alternating,

a few sips forgotten—

what you're consuming

is *shared narrative space*.

It's not the drink that satisfies.

It's the feeling of being seen.

Of not performing.

Of watching someone else remember who
they are

in your gaze.

The coffee table becomes an interface.

The pauses between sentences become sacred.

And if the coffee tastes good,

it's only because the moment is held well.

The Ritual Beneath the Ritual

You think you're just catching up.

But you're actually running a protocol—

one that checks:

- *Are we still safe with each other?*
- *Do you still listen the way I remember?*
- *Can I still speak freely, or have our scripts hardened?*

You think it's casual.

But it's an audit of connection.

And coffee is the symbolic object

you both agree to hold

so you don't have to say:

"This matters."

Framing the Moment Without Saying It

You don't frame a coffee date by explaining it.

You frame it by how you show up.

- Do you reach for your phone?
- Do you drink too fast, as if the cup is a task?
- Do your eyes wander more than your thoughts?
- Or do you stay, in presence—without agenda?

The way you sit.

The way you listen.

The way you smile, or nod, or let silence stretch—

That's the real brew.

It's not the roast or the origin.

It's not the beans or the barista.

It's you.

And how you choose to be here.

Fully.

Shared Time, Not Shared Drink

If someone asked what you had,

you might say:

"Oh, just a cappuccino."

But that's not true.

You had a moment where someone leaned in.

You had a small oasis in a fractured day.

You had the luxury of unscattered attention.

You had an interface that held two selves without rush.

That's what you really drank.

A cup filled with shared awareness.

And that's why it felt good.

Even if the coffee was mediocre.

You Don't Remember the Beans

You'll forget the brand.

The taste.

Maybe even the name of the café.

But you won't forget how the other person

was in that moment.

Did they really listen?

Did they soften?

Did they meet you there, in the same sip of time?

We don't archive flavors.

We archive feelings.

And the best coffee dates

are the ones where the feeling stays warm—

long after the mug goes cold.

5.3 Two People, One Brew, Different Worlds

Even shared cups hold irreconcilable experiences.

You both ordered the same thing.

Two cups.

Same beans.

Same roast.

Same barista.

You sip.

They sip.

And still—

you're not drinking the same coffee.

Because what enters your mouth isn't just liquid.

It's meaning.

A Cup Is Never Just a Cup

Even when identical in form,

a cup of coffee enters two lives with different stories.

To you, that cappuccino might taste like comfort.

To them, it might taste like compromise.

To you, the bitterness might feel grounding.

To them, it might sting like a memory they thought they buried.

You think you're sharing a moment.

But you're really co-existing in parallel interpretations.

And no amount of nodding or "Mmm, good right?"

can close that gap completely.

Because taste isn't just physical.

It's autobiographical.

Your Tongue is a Translator of Experience

Every sip is filtered through years of association:

- Childhood mornings filled with the smell of instant granules.
- A breakup that started over brunch.
- The first time you traveled alone and ordered a macchiato in broken Italian.
- A burnt pot of coffee during an all-nighter that changed your life.

So even now, as you both sip the same brew,

your bodies aren't just reacting to caffeine and acidity—

they're interpreting a lifetime of echoes.

The cup is one.

But the experience is not.

Misreading the Shared Moment

This is where many people trip.

They assume that "drinking together" means "feeling the same."

But parallel presence doesn't mean mutual perception.

You might be softening into the warmth of the cup,

while the other person is tightening behind their smile.

You might be seeing connection,

while they're performing comfort.

Not out of malice.

But because even when we meet,

we bring our ghosts.

And sometimes, they drink too.

Shared Time ≠ Shared Reality

This is the hard truth of togetherness:

proximity doesn't guarantee resonance.

You can share a table,

share a story,

even share a dream—

and still live in separate perceptual
dimensions.

The cup between you becomes

a fragile interface—

not a merger.

And yet, we keep reaching for it.

Because even imperfect overlap

feels better than full solitude.

Don't Mistake Divergence for Disconnection

Just because they taste something different

doesn't mean they aren't here with you.

Difference isn't distance.

You can name your tasting notes—

nutty, floral, rich, balanced—

and they might smile politely, not tasting any of that.

And yet, if they're listening,

if they're staying,

if they're letting your experience matter

even when it isn't theirs—

that is connection.

Not matching flavors.

But holding space for non-overlapping truths.

145

When the Brew Reveals the Boundary

Sometimes, though,

you'll hit a harder wall.

You'll say, "Isn't this beautiful?"

and they'll shrug.

You'll say, "Doesn't this taste like home?"

and they'll flinch.

You'll pour your perception

into the center of the table—

and it won't land.

That's not failure.

That's a mirror.

Coffee didn't cause the distance.

It revealed it.

So Why Still Share It?

Because even in misalignment,

there's still something sacred.

Two people—

rooted in separate worlds—

choosing, even briefly,

to orbit around a common cup.

It's not about harmony.

It's about willingness.

To be there.

To stay.

To drink anyway.

Even if what warms you

doesn't warm them the same.

5.4 The Grinder at 7AM

Sound, like scent, is how we feel space existing.

The First Thing You Hear

You're still half-asleep when it starts.

That low rumble, sharp whirl—

the grinder turns beans into fragments,

and the fragments into ritual.

Before any scent reaches your nose,

before the cup touches your lips,

there is sound.

The grind *marks the beginning*—

not just of brewing,

but of being.

Because in that moment,

you are reminded:

you exist within a world that moves before you do.

Noise as Atmosphere

We usually treat sound as background—

something to filter, ignore, or shut out.

But some sounds do the opposite.

They *shape* the room.

The grinder at 7AM isn't noise.

It's presence.

It gives structure to the silence.

It sketches the edges of your home.

It tells you: *you are in a life that is happening*.

Not in theory.

Not as potential.

But in motion—gritty, physical, loud.

149

It's the world reminding you it's still here.

Auditory Anchors

Scent gets more attention when we talk about memory.

But sound has its own power.

The whistle of a kettle.

The hiss of the steam wand.

The final thump of the moka pot lid as pressure settles.

These aren't just auditory cues.

They're emotional punctuation.

They mark transitions from thought to action,

from waking to doing,

from inner to outer.

And they do it *without words*.

Sound as a Shared Interface

When you grind beans,

you're not just preparing coffee.

You're declaring:

Something is about to happen.

Your partner hears it in the bedroom.

Your neighbor hears it through thin walls.

Even your cat knows—it's time.

A small machine in the kitchen

becomes a distributed signal system

across physical and relational space.

What's fascinating is:

we rarely acknowledge it.

But we feel it.

We act in response to it.

We organize our lives around it.

The Performance of Everyday Machinery

Now flip the scene.

You walk into someone else's home.

It's early.

You hear the grinder before you see them.

Immediately, a feeling enters your body.

A sense of rhythm.

Of welcome.

Of being let into the prelude of their day.

You haven't said hello.

You haven't shared a word.

But the sound _is_ the greeting.

It says:

This is my pace. This is my space. You're in it now, too.

And suddenly,

you are not a guest.

You are part of a flow already in motion.

<u>Ritual Has a Sound</u>

Modern life tends to sterilize mornings.

Phones. Screens. Quiet cars. Noise-cancelled trains.

But coffee, especially when ground fresh,

refuses to be silent.

It hums. It scratches. It interrupts.

And that interruption is a *gift*.

Because it reminds you:

you are not just an interface of inputs.

You are a being in space,

framed by vibrations.

Your heartbeat joins the rhythm.

Your breath meets the motor.

153

And somehow,

you feel *present*.

Listening as Belonging

Here's the meta-layer you rarely name:

You don't just listen to sound.

You *recognize yourself through it.*

If you hear the grinder and it soothes you,

it means you've made peace with slowness.

If it annoys you,

maybe you're resisting rhythm.

If you don't hear it at all anymore,

maybe you've stopped noticing the stage
your life plays out on.

But the moment you do—

even for a second—

you reenter your life through your ears.

Sound reminds you of your real dimensions.

It says:

You are not abstract. You are in a room. Right now. With gravity. With heat. With noise.

And that, too,

is a kind of awakening.

5.5 The Mug You Always Choose

Familiar objects are anchors of identity.

The Pattern You Didn't Question

You open the cabinet.

Six mugs stare back at you.

Different colors, shapes, sizes—some gifted, some bought on trips, one chipped but still loved.

And yet, every morning, your hand moves toward *that one*.

Not because you deliberated. Not because it's objectively better.

But because something about it feels like *you*.

Most people don't realize they have a favorite mug.

They think they rotate. They believe they're flexible.

But patterns always reveal themselves.

And every pattern holds a story.

The mug you always choose is not just about convenience or comfort.

It's about *continuity*—a daily anchor in a world of shifting noise.

Objects as Self-Stabilizers

We like to believe identity is internal— something we hold in our mind, our character, our values.

But the self is also *externalized*.

It lives in routines. In chosen tools. In daily interfaces.

Your mug isn't just an object.

It's a feedback loop.

Every time you hold it, you reinforce a version of yourself you recognize.

It might be minimalist.

It might be handmade.

It might be branded from a company whose mission aligns with yours.

Or maybe it's just heavy in a way that grounds you.

That familiarity is not passive.

It's actively *performative*.

You don't just use the mug.

You *confirm yourself* with it.

The Inheritance of Association

Maybe your mug is white and clean.

You associate it with focus. With quiet mornings. With clarity.

Maybe it's brightly colored and chipped.

You associate it with warmth, imperfection, resilience.

Maybe it was given to you by someone you no longer talk to.

And yet, it remains—because even broken relationships leave meaningful rituals behind.

The point isn't sentimentality.

It's structure.

The mug becomes a container not just of liquid,

but of *memory, context, emotional design.*

You didn't just choose it once.

You keep choosing it.

And that repetition builds layers—layers that feel like *truth*.

But they're not universal truths.

They're *you-shaped* truths.

The Invisible Design of Ritual

When people redesign their lives, they often overlook objects.

They chase big changes—move cities, change jobs, shift schedules.

But the strongest patterns are anchored in *small defaults*.

A mug.

A table spot.

A drawer you always avoid.

These hold *structural memory*.

They script the edges of your presence.

The mug you always choose isn't just about taste.

It's about *recognizability*.

You trust the feeling of your fingers wrapping around it.

You like the way it holds heat.

You know exactly how full it needs to be to match your first sip preference.

It's a choreography that tells your body:

We've done this before. We know this version of the world.

And so, you begin.

The Meta of Material Familiarity

Pause here.

You didn't just learn something about coffee.

You learned something about how you stabilize identity.

Through shape. Through rhythm. Through selection.

This is not about materialism.

This is about *material mediation*.

The world doesn't just reflect who you are.

161

It *shapes how you show up*.

And when you pick a familiar mug,

you're not avoiding variety.

You're building a recognizable interface to begin your day from.

It's not a limitation.

It's a *re-entry point* into coherence.

The mug is a signal.

To yourself.

To your morning.

To your pace.

To your interpretation of what this day might mean.

Every Ritual Has an Entry Point

In the end, coffee wasn't the topic.

It was the medium.

Through it, you've explored taste, self-perception, friction, memory, and time.

But none of that matters

—unless it lands back in the body.

The mug you always choose *is* the landing.

It's where abstraction finds temperature.

Where thought becomes sip.

Where ritual becomes *real*.

You don't need to change your mug.

You just need to know:

It's already saying something about you.

And if one day, you reach for a different one—

maybe that's not just a mood.

Maybe that's the start of a new *you*.

Part VI: After the Sip

What stays is not the taste—but what it moved inside you.

The cup is empty.

The flavor has faded.

But something remains.

It's not the note of citrus or the trace of bitterness on your tongue.

It's not even the memory of the brew itself.

It's the shift that happened *while* it was there.

The slight reorientation in how you met your morning,

or how you paused longer than usual between sips.

Coffee, like any ritual, is not just about the moment it occupies.

It's about what it unlocks—afterward.

In the silence.

In the breath you took without noticing.

In the thought that lingered when the mug was already rinsed.

This final part is not a summary.

It's a soft return.

Not to where you were—

but to a version of you that's been quietly rewritten

one cup at a time.

Not because of what you tasted.

But because of what the tasting allowed.

6.1 The Cup Wasn't the Point

The act was a portal, not a goal.

You brewed it.

You sat with it.

You drank it.

And now—it's gone.

But something lingers.

Not on your lips.

Not even in your memory.

But in the quiet shift of *something* that no longer fits the same way it did before.

We often mistake rituals for their results.

We think the point of coffee is the caffeine.

The wakefulness.

The flavor.

The satisfaction of checking a box in the morning that says *I've started my day.*

But rituals don't work like that.

They're not designed to deliver something.

They're designed to *change* something.

Quietly. Subtly. Invisibly.

And the cup?

That was just the interface.

A container through which the act could move.

The taste was only the surface tension—the gateway, not the destination.

Because what really happened wasn't in the cup.

It was in *you*.

In how you sat with it today versus yesterday.

In what you thought about while it cooled.

In the words you almost texted—but didn't.

In the feeling you remembered before it faded again.

In the way you placed the mug down slower than usual, as if something asked to be left intact.

The mistake we often make is assigning meaning to outcomes—

The brew was "good."

The flavor was "off."

167

The texture was "perfect."

We treat experience like performance.

But the truth is, not everything meaningful has to show up as *memorable*.

The meaning lives in the shift.

The frame that quietly changed without announcement.

The mood that softened.

The pace that slowed.

The thought that didn't defend itself quite as quickly.

You won't write it down.

You won't post about it.

You might not even remember it happened.

But it did.

The ritual passed through you.

Not to impress.

Not to achieve.

But to *recalibrate*.

To remind your system that not all inputs are transactional.

Some are transformational—precisely because they never declared themselves as such.

You could've skipped this one.

You could've bought a different one.

You could've made it faster, fancier, more photogenic.

But instead, you let it be what it was.

And by doing so, *you let yourself* be what you were.

Not optimized.

Not improved.

Just present enough for a portal to open.

And humble enough not to force it closed.

That was the point.

Not the cup.

Not the contents.

But the quiet access it offered.

You walked through it.

Even if you didn't realize you did.

6.2 What You Thought You'd Taste Wasn't There

Disappointment reveals the structure of your expectation.

You brought it to your lips with a quiet kind of confidence.

You thought you knew.

You had a picture in your head—a memory, a desire, a promise.

You sipped.

And it wasn't that.

Not even close.

Was it worse? Not necessarily.

Just *other*.

Unexpected. Out of sync. Off.

And because it didn't fit the frame you brought to it, your mind labeled it *wrong*.

Bad.

A mistake.

But what if it wasn't the cup that failed you?

What if it was your frame?

We rarely taste anything in isolation.

Every bite, every sip, is shadowed by memory—of past experiences, of cultural stories, of yesterday's version that was somehow *just right*.

We don't just approach a flavor with curiosity.

We approach it with a script.

And when the flavor doesn't follow the lines, we don't question the script.

We blame the brew.

Disappointment, then, isn't always a comment on quality.

It's a signal.

A bright, flashing indicator of *what we expected without noticing that we expected it*.

You didn't say it out loud, but part of you believed:

- This roast should be fruitier.
- This milk should be silkier.
- This café should know what you like without asking.
- This moment should feel like the last one.

And so, when it didn't...

The feeling wasn't just "not good."

It was *misaligned*.

A minor betrayal of an unspoken mental map.

But here's the shift:

What if that map—your internal structure of how things *should* taste, feel, unfold—

...was never updated?

Never truly examined?

Most of our preferences are accumulations.

We inherit them.

We layer them unconsciously.

We collect them from others, from media, from half-remembered praise or childhood treats.

And we rarely stop to ask: *Where did this taste even come from?*

So the next time the cup feels like a letdown—

Pause.

Not to fix the brew.

But to trace the shape of your assumption.

What were you chasing?

Whose voice was echoing in your anticipation?

Was the flavor actually flawed—or was it just unfamiliar to the version of you that made the decision?

Disappointment can be sharp.

But it's also precise.

It shows you the edges of your unconscious criteria.

It illuminates the invisible contract you wrote before the cup even reached your hands.

That is a gift.

Because once you see the outline,

You can redraw it.

You can ask whether it still fits.

You can ask whether you want to taste what's *there*,

...or keep hunting for what never was.

The cup didn't fail.

It simply didn't audition for the role you cast it in.

So what now?

You can discard it.

You can chase another.

175

Or—you can stay.

Stay in the discomfort of misalignment.

Stay with the flavor that resists your prediction.

Stay long enough to realize that maybe...

what you *expected* was never actually what you *needed*.

And in that stay, something opens.

A willingness to rewrite your sensory grammar.

A quiet respect for what's different, not lesser.

And the courage to meet the world as it is—

Not as your past told you it should be.

6.3 Some Brews Were Never Meant for You

Not liking something can be an act of clarity, not failure.

You tried.

You really did.

You listened to the praise.

You heard the words people used—*balanced, sophisticated, complex.*

You watched them close their eyes after each sip as if tasting some secret that you had yet to earn.

You thought, *Maybe I just need to grow into it.*

Maybe my taste isn't ready.

Maybe I'm the one who's missing something.

So you gave it another try.

You sipped slower.

177

You read about it, asked questions, adjusted the water temperature, bought the right grinder.

Still—no magic. No click.

It didn't taste *bad*. But it didn't feel *right*.

And quietly, beneath all that effort, another thought whispered itself into the back of your mind:

Is it okay to walk away from a flavor that everyone else seems to love?

Yes.

It is not only okay.

It is necessary.

Because knowing what you don't like isn't failure.

It's definition.

We're taught to treat distaste as a shortcoming—like our inability to appreciate something beautiful reveals a gap in our refinement.

But what if dislike is just your system telling the truth?

What if *no* is not resistance, but resonance?

Not every brew carries your rhythm.

Not every origin is your home.

Not every roast speaks your language.

And that's not a limitation of you, or of it.

It's just a signal: you're not a match.

Discomfort isn't always a lesson.

Sometimes it's a boundary.

Sometimes it's the quiet voice that protects your time, your energy, your attention— from being poured endlessly into things that were never going to nourish you.

In a world that romanticizes endurance— learning to stay, to stretch, to develop your palate—there's something radical about letting go.

To admit: *This isn't for me.*

And to stop.

You're not giving up.

You're becoming clear.

Because presence doesn't require universal appreciation.

It requires *honest alignment*.

And that means building a taste that's yours—not curated to impress, not borrowed to belong, not tolerated in the name of self-improvement.

The world will offer you endless brews.

Each one crafted with intention, history, care.

But that doesn't obligate you to drink all of them.

Respect can exist without agreement.

You can bow to the craftsmanship of something you never wish to sip again.

And here's the quiet meta-truth:

Knowing what isn't yours is a deeper kind of intimacy than chasing what might be.

Because the moment you release what doesn't resonate,

You begin to make room for what does.

You begin to hear the subtler tones of your own orientation.

You stop asking, *What should I like?*

And start asking, *What actually lands? What actually moves something in me?*

This doesn't mean you should close yourself off to challenge, to novelty, to friction.

But there's a difference between curiosity and self-erasure.

Between stretching your edges and denying your center.

Some brews aren't yours.

And that's not a judgment.

It's a map.

One that helps you find the cups that are.

The ones that fit your silence.

The ones that make you feel seen.

Not because they're perfect—

But because they're true.

6.4 You're Not Tasting Beans. You're Tasting Stories

Every origin, every roast, every process carries human decisions.

You think it's just a cup.

Hot liquid, dark roast, maybe a note of citrus or chocolate.

You sip. You judge. You move on.

But nothing in that cup is neutral.

Every drop has passed through hundreds of choices, made by hands you'll never meet.

Choices about climate, altitude, varietal.

Choices about when to harvest, how to wash, how long to dry.

Choices about whether to ship the beans green, or to roast them on-site.

Choices about how dark to go, how fast to heat, when to stop.

And then—your own choices: grind size, brew time, water temperature, vessel.

You are never just tasting beans.

You are tasting the **entire path** of how something came to be.

Every cup is an archive of invisible intentions.

A farmer in Ethiopia let the cherries hang a day longer on the tree.

A cooperative in Guatemala shifted from washed to natural process.

A roaster in Tokyo tested three profiles before deciding this batch would go a little deeper, bring out the tobacco note.

You weren't there.

But the cup remembers.

And when you taste it—really taste it— you're not decoding flavor.

You're meeting **structure**.

Structure that someone else shaped.

Structure that whispers: *this is how we decided it should be.*

Structure that sometimes aligns with your taste, and sometimes doesn't.

But either way, it's a story.

Taste, in that sense, is never purely yours.

It's a point of intersection—where your perceptual system meets someone else's framing.

Your palate isn't discovering a truth hidden inside the bean.

It's interpreting a **narrative** encoded in chemistry.

Which means: *your judgment is also part of the story.*

You're not just the audience.

You're the co-author of what the coffee becomes.

Because no story lives without a reader.

And no cup lives without a taster.

185

What you call "flavor" is memory, context, and design colliding in a moment.

That note of almond?

Maybe it only exists because you had marzipan at your grandmother's house.

That sense of "clarity"?

Maybe it's because you've grown accustomed to filtered experiences.

That bitterness you reject?

Maybe it's not the coffee at all—it's your history with discomfort.

You think you're tasting the bean.

But you're really tasting your **relation** to the world that shaped it.

Which is why two people can sip the same cup, and walk away with two entirely different truths.

One says, *It's bold and complex.*

The other says, *It's sour and confusing.*

186

They're both right.

Because flavor doesn't just describe the object.

It reveals the **interface** between story and self.

And sometimes, the most profound part of that interface is the moment you realize:

Someone cared enough to shape this experience for a stranger they'd never meet.

They picked the cherry by hand.

They tested the roast curve ten times.

They believed—quietly, insistently—that **someone out there** would be moved.

Not just by the caffeine, or even by the flavor.

But by the act itself.

This is what makes coffee different from commodity.

It carries the fingerprint of choice.

187

Not just efficiency.

Not just replication.

But deliberate framing of what matters.

A choice to pursue brightness over body.

A choice to lean into funk, or to round out the edge.

A choice to take a risk—on you.

So the next time you sip something that moves you, pause.

Not to praise the roast.

Not to name the note.

But to notice: *there is a human somewhere inside this flavor.*

A hand you will never shake.

A story you were never meant to know.

And yet—somehow—you did.

Because the story didn't need words.

It only needed a vessel.

And you were willing to taste.

6.5 The Cup You Left Half Full

What's unfinished still carries presence. Maybe more than what's done.

The sip you didn't take.

The warmth that faded while you looked away, distracted by a message, a thought, a task.

The cup that cooled beside you—not out of disrespect, but because life continued moving—and so did you.

We often treat what's unfinished as failure.

A half-read book. A conversation that never found closure.

A project paused, indefinitely.

Or a cup of coffee that didn't reach your lips again.

But maybe we've misunderstood what "completion" means.

Maybe the cup's meaning doesn't live in its empty bottom.

Maybe its **presence** outlives its consumption.

Because presence doesn't always demand closure.

Sometimes, it only asks for *recognition*— that this moment happened,

and left something in you, even if you didn't drain it dry.

What you leave behind is not always abandonment. Sometimes, it's a quiet boundary.

You didn't finish the cup—not because you didn't care,

but because *that was enough*.

Because a sip held the insight.

Because a taste said what it needed to say.

Because the experience reached a point where your internal signal whispered, *we're done here*—even if the cup was not.

This, too, is presence.

It takes awareness to notice the moment *before* habit pushes you to finish.

To realize: **not all wholes need to be consumed.**

In fact, some of the most meaningful rituals are those left slightly open—unfinished by design,

not because they lack value, but because they trust your internal closure more than external symmetry.

The coffee that's left is not waste.

It's a memory anchor.

A soft reminder that you were here.

That something happened.

That time flowed through this mug, and a version of you met it.

There's dignity in the half-full.

Not in the optimistic cliché, but in the structural honesty it reveals:

Life is made of fragments.

Not every story gets a neat ending.

Not every conversation will circle back.

Not every encounter will reach its full arc.

And yet—what's partial is not lesser.

Sometimes, it's more *alive*.

Because what's unfinished keeps echoing.

It holds space for reinterpretation.

It resists finality—and in doing so, it invites return.

The half-full cup on your desk might call you tomorrow.

Not to reheat it.

Not to resume what you started.

But to **remember**.

193

To remember that in the middle of everything,

you paused.

You noticed.

You met yourself, briefly.

And then, you moved on—without erasing the trace.

Completion is not the same as meaning.

We live in a world obsessed with finish lines.

Complete the task. Drink the cup. Check the box.

But coffee was never a checklist.

It was a **threshold**.

An entrance to awareness.

A framing device for presence.

A way to meet the ordinary with a different lens.

And so, what remains in that half-full mug is not failure.

It's a testament.

That you allowed yourself to begin,

and didn't force yourself to end.

That you knew when the conversation turned internal.

That you sensed when the moment shifted.

That you gave yourself permission to *stop*,

without erasing the significance of what already happened.

In this way, the unfinished becomes sacred.

Not because it lacked time—

but because it held exactly what was needed,

then let the rest unfold elsewhere.

So leave the last sip, if you must.

Let it stay.

As a quiet symbol of a truth many miss:

Meaning doesn't always come from what's finished. Sometimes, it lives in what you had the courage to leave undone.

About the Author

Kingfai Au, also known as Fai, is not a barista. Not a coffee expert. Not a connoisseur.

He's simply someone who never stopped paying attention.

Every morning, he brews his own cup—not out of ritual, but out of rhythm. In the quiet swirl of steam and bitterness, he began to notice something: the way coffee reflected his pace, his preferences, his shifting states of self.

This book didn't come from mastery. It came from *noticing*—the kind that accumulates over hundreds of quiet mornings, where the same cup never quite feels the same. Where taste becomes texture, and texture becomes thought.

Fai's writings often emerge from these lived patterns. As a systems thinker, he explores how meaning forms—not just in frameworks, but in daily gestures. His books aren't answers, but invitations. Not manuals, but mirrors.

When he writes, he isn't trying to explain coffee.

He's tracing the outlines of presence through it.

Fai lives in Tokyo, builds systems by day, and questions them by night. He still doesn't think he's a "coffee person." But he knows that when something makes you return every day—not out of habit, but out of *attention*—it's worth writing about.

Website: www.aukingfai.com

Before You
Close This Book

Thank you—for letting these pages sit quietly beside your mornings, your thoughts, or whatever part of you was willing to listen.

This book was never meant to teach you about coffee.

It was an invitation.

To see more.

To feel more honestly.

To pause—not just before the next sip, but before the next assumption, the next autopilot hour.

Coffee, in these pages, was never the subject. It was the interface. A companion. A slow signal that said: *you are here*. And in noticing how you meet the cup, you may begin to notice how you meet the rest of your life.

199

If something stirred while reading—
curiosity, discomfort, presence—that's more
than enough.

Because this was never about beans, or
brewers, or the best roast.

It was about awareness.

Fai writes across themes of perception,
cognitive framing, emotional presence, and
the quiet architectures of daily life. Coffee is
just one entry point. There are others—
books not about the thing, but about what
the thing unlocks.

So if you're still sensing something—
unfinished, expanding, awake—stay
connected.

There's more ahead.

And maybe, somewhere in a different city, a
different hour, we'll meet again—over
another cup.

Warmly,

Fai

Printed in Dunstable, United Kingdom